Boxes, Tins and Balls

Jon said,

"We can play a game

with the boxes,

the tins,

and the balls.

They can all go into this bag."

"You can go first, Sally," said Jon.

"Can you find the little box?

You can not look inside the bag."

Sally put her hand

into the bag.

"Look!" said Sally.

"Here is the little box."

Sally put the little box
back into the bag.
She said to Matthew,
"Can you find the big tin?"

Matthew put his hand into the bag.

"I can't find the big tin," he said.

"Where is it?"

"Oh, yes," said Matthew.

"I **can** find the big tin!

Here it is."

Matthew put the big tin
back into the bag.

He said,

"Can you find the little ball, Jon?"

"Look!" said Jon.

"This is the little ball."

Jon put the little ball
back into the bag.

"I like this game," he said.
"We can play it again."

a little box   a big box

a little tin   a big tin

a little ball   a big ball